CLOSE

CLOSE

Draw Near

Benton T. Thompson, III

Cover design by Daniel Thompson

Published by:

McDougal & Associates
18896 Greenwell Springs Road
Greenwell Springs, LA 70739
www.thepublishedword.com

ISBN 978-1-950398-22-5

Printed on demand in the U.S., the U.K. and Australia

For Worldwide Distribution

Books by
Benton T. Thompson, III

Dedication

I dedicate this work to others who have been heartbroken over the loss of a loved one or anyone who suffers from a deep hurt of any kind. My hurt was over the loss of my sister. It was very devastating for me to lose her. I was really hurt, I missed her so much every day, and I didn't know where to turn or who to talk to about it.

I didn't want to talk with just anyone; I wanted to talk to someone who could understand my pain, someone who knew me and knew her, who knew us.

It was tough every day just to keep going, a challenge to manage to get through each day. Sometimes I couldn't see myself making it through a whole day; I had to take it hour by hour. There were days when I thought perhaps this was all just a dream, and other days when I wished it were.

Eventually, I began a "grateful journal" as a way to stay sane. Each day I would try to find one positive takeaway from the day just to keep me going. Some days I was grateful just for the sun being out. Other days I was grateful for a cool breeze. I tried to find something, anything to maintain my hope that things could and would get better than the day before.

I did have some things to occur that I could actually cheer about. But there were many days I just had to keep believing that things would one day be okay. I couldn't yet believe that they would be "better," but I could believe for "okay."

I would never forget my sister, nor did I want to. I just didn't want to hurt anymore because she was no longer with me. I couldn't call her, see her or laugh with her like we used to do. There was nothing. It was all gone. All I had were the memories of what had been.

I continued writing in my grateful journal for a whole year. Then gradually, day by day, bit by bit, I found that I wasn't as depressed as I had been. Each day I continued to make myself write down at least one thing to be thankful for. On the really good days, I had more than one thing to be thankful for.

The best thing was that each day I was being drawn CLOSE. I still missed my sister, of course, but at least her absence was not always so painful. And I am believing the same thing for you: that one day you will find peace and hope. My prayer is that you, too, will be drawn in CLOSE as you read the following pages. So, I dedicate this book to YOU!

Introduction

What is this book about? Close, as the name would seem to suggest, is about proximity, not in the sense of a relational closeness, but rather that which is born from the will, a desire to be close to what or who you are pursuing. Close must be felt and not just read. Hold it close to you as you read. Hold its concepts close as you listen with your heart to every word.

From a very high level perspective in which things seem large and obvious, close would appear to be about a well-known, familiar and oftentimes controversial historical figure. How we view this figure can vary greatly on the spectrum from fraud to hero, or from fictional to unrealistic. Other viewpoints might vary from merely man's imagination to an overly glorified ideal. However you view this character, remember it only appears to be just about them from a very high level. But as you look further and "closer" into this work, you will see it from many other viewpoints.

Some viewpoints might appear cold and familiar, while others might seem unknown, vulnerable and yet excitingly desirable. From a certain perspective, this book might be seen as being about human relationships at its basic core, a person's desire to feel connected to the world in which they live and those who share it with them. No one wants to feel left out or disconnected. Regardless of our differences, in many ways we are all somewhat alike. We all have needs and desires. The message to be found here is one of inclusion rather than exclusion.

Close is about a journey through time, life and experiences. While it seems to just focus on a few central characters, there are plenty of other bystanders who can teach us all many valuable lessons. Make sure you hear their voices. This work is not about religion, but rather about relationship—a relationship between a man and a woman, mankind and nature, friends and detractors. As you read and feel this book, you might experience a variety of emotions and sensations that will impact your soul. Allow yourself permission to feel what you feel unashamedly.

Close is about space and spacing. It is to that end that I have written the book with space for you to express your thoughts and feelings after each sentence or emotion as they are occurring. I didn't want to cram a word or thought into every bit of white space available. You have been given space to think, feel and write. So relax and experience being close. Most of all, I believe you will find this to be a good smooth read, full of mystery, history and intrigue.

As you read, allow yourself to be drawn in CLOSE.

Close to your friends.

Close to your beliefs.

Close to yourself.

Get ready to experience feeling Close!

Benton T. Thompson, III

Mount Hermon

~1~

Halfway Around the World

Prepare yourself to go with me on a journey, far, far away. Clear your mind of all the events of the day, so we can head off. Picture yourself in a very hot and dry place, a barren area of landscape where little precipitation occurs and living conditions are both hostile and harmful for plant and animal life alike. Above you see the blazing hot sun, with little or no breeze. The humidity almost takes your breath away, and your lungs labor to pull in fresh air. If you think we're in the desert, then you are correct.

About a third of the surface of the entire world is arid or semi-arid, with desert-like conditions. Wind-blown sand grains strike against any object that moves. Rocks are smoothed down and glazed over, and the wind sorts the sand in a uniform deposit known as sand dunes.

People have struggled to live in deserts and their surrounding regions for thousands of years. But there is a place in a particular desert that may actually seem like a mirage. It looks like a wonderful oasis, but what your eyes will see is true. It's a place so beautiful, so majestic, so vibrant, so lush and so full of life, a glorious oasis right in the middle of the arid desert, with large majestic trees, bountiful orchards and thick, bushy shrubs, vibrant tropical plants and emerald green ferns interspersed with wonderful brightly-colored wildflowers everywhere you look.

Try to smell the intoxicating aroma of one of the desert's most prized stars, the Lavender Mountain Lily, as it fills your nostrils. Can you smell them? All the beautiful and rare butterflies that are here love them. You can see these creatures fluttering around everywhere, light and free. All things here receive nourishment from the rolling streams and rivers that flow throughout the mountainside, weaving in and out along the slopes, creating magnificent waterfalls that drop into deep pools of timeless and mysterious water.

All of this rests on the backs of age-old mountains of earth and rock that form a tropical paradise high above the desert floor, a place where rare and exotic wildlife roam freely—like the Syrian brown bear, the Arabian oryx (a medium-sized antelope), the Asiatic lion and cheetah, the wild ass and the Nubian ibex (a wild goat). You can also see rabbits, gazelles, wolves, badgers, jackals, wildcats and an extremely uncommon leopard or two.

CLOSE

All types of birds are there as well: eagles, storks, vultures, hawks, doves, ravens, various types of sparrows, blackbirds, larks and starlings. Where in the world could you find something like this? It's right there in the middle of all this vastness, just standing there, mighty and proud, waiting and watching over the desert plains. It is a huge mountain range that juts high into the sky above all the earth and can be seen from miles and miles around. Its mountaintops are so tall and so pronounced they could have been used as stepping stones for God Himself to come down from Heaven to Earth and visit with the local inhabitants.

~*~

White snow-capped peaks pierce into the heavens, while the basin is cloaked in a misty fog. As the sun shines brightly on the glaciered tops, a halo of fog and mist form just below its peaks, and so it is with this wonderful mountainous region that is full of mystery, intrigue and history. The fog covers the rich, flowing ecosystem with exotic wildlife, and streams and rivers feed throughout the region, as well as deep dark mysteries.

Could this be a real place? Is it just a legend? Perhaps an old wives tale? Or maybe a truth so far above our imagination one could hardly believe it were true. But, yes, it is a real place, a mystical area in which fog is a regular guest in the dry desert heat. Many tales have been told about this mountain, some familiar, others not so much. It was called the "Snowy Mountain," but it may be better known by its commonly-recognized name—Mount Hermon.

The Hermon mountain range in current-day Lebanon sprawls more than ninety miles across the plains, with three distinct summits, each measuring the same height. Because of its great height, Mount Hermon gets a lot of precipitation, and its runoff forms streams and rivers that feed into other mighty rivers and lakes.

There has been a lot written about Mount Hermon, but still very little is really known about it.

As the dew of Hermon

that descended upon

the mountains of Zion.

So the dews on Hermon's hill

which the summer clouds distil,

floating southward in the night,

pearly gems on Zion's light!

—William Digby Seymour

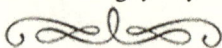

This is the place where the Lord Himself is recorded as commanding an eternal blessing to rest upon it, "even life for evermore."

The eyes of the auspicious Mount Hermon could see everywhere, or so it seemed to the locals, as it covered more than five thousand acres of countryside. It could be seen by all of the residents and their neighbors in the surrounding areas. Mount Hermon towers more than nine thousand feet above sea level. That's more than eight Empire State buildings tall. From the top of it, if you look due west, you can see Beirut, Lebanon, as well as Sidon and Tyre. Looking even further westward, one can see the beautiful, serene, blue waters of the majestic Mediterranean Sea.

Turn southwest, and you can see Nazareth and the Sea of Galilee and, in the distance, the old city of Jerusalem.

As you pivot to face eastward, you can see Damascus, Syria. And if you look straight up, you can see the mist from the fog curtains that hide the very entrance to Heaven itself—hypothetically speaking, of course.

Mount Hermon is right in the epicenter of it all. Everyone knew of Hermon, and Hermon knew of everyone.

~*~

Being seated at the foot of Hermon in the Golan Heights early in the morning, you can probably visualize how water could condense from the thick fog and then run down the face of this mighty mountainside to the awaiting thick, lush forest floor below, spreading out to the widest ravines, descending into the evening moonlight as a heavy dew cloud, covering the night, as its sprawls throughout the land, only to rise in the morning and begin the adventure all over again.

Hermon, with its white crown of snow, is quite awe-inspiring as it glistens during the day with the backdrop of the hot desert sun as an unlikely but faithful companion. Hermon and the desert have a very symbiotic relationship. Hermon needs the aridness to feed the tropics, and the desert needs the precipitation to quench its thirst. The juxtaposed view of this lush mountain sanctuary in the middle of the vast wilderness is truly amazing. As in life, sometimes we receive the best gifts from the most unlikely sources, and when we least expect it. Nowhere in the whole Middle East is there a view as spectacular as this one. That's why so many spoke of its unfailing beauty.

The Mountain sat upon the plain

In his tremendous chair,

His observation omnifold,

His inquest everywhere.

The seasons played around his knees

Like children round a sire.

Grandfather of the Days is he,

Of dawn, the ancestor!

—Emily Dickerson

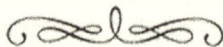

Six Hundred Miles Away

Hermon has long played a major role in the lives of all those in the surrounding communities, its constant presence and beauty always giving reassurance to any and all onlookers. Its steadfastness has resonated a peace within the soul that was hard to explain or forget. But Hermon added far more than just esthetic value; it also provided a lifeline to communities on all sides of it.

As noted, the dew from Mount Hermon was enough to create streams and rivers on and around its mountainsides, which, in turn, flowed into the Jordan River, from there into the Sea of Galilee and coming out of the Sea of Galilee again entering the Jordan that flowed down through the Jordan Valley, feeding all the people in the region.

The waters from Hermon even flowed into the great city of Jerusalem. Although there is no river in Jerusalem today, it is believed that the springs running deep beneath the city have their source on Mount Hermon.

Jerusalem is a city well known for its great festivals. Imagine a grand festival for a grand mountain. What would that look like—the Mount Hermon Festival, with all its glory and spectacle, widely publicized and always eagerly anticipated? Nobody knows how to throw a better party than Jerusalem, adorned with all the pomp and circumstance you could ever want. People should plan to stay for days and enjoy every minute of their time there.

Anything that you could have possibly wanted would have been at the Hermon Festival. Everything that Hermon helped to bring forth would be on display: wines of all types, a variety of cheeses, breads, fruits, vegetables, livestock, meat and fish. Fish was always the most celebrated menu item, given all the water in and around the Jordan Valley and the fact that most people there were fishermen by trade.

The festival also gave the fishermen a chance to show off a bit, a contest to see who had the most entertaining account of "the big one that got away," to win the Bragging Rights Trophy. No matter their ethnicity, whether rich or poor, old or young, both near and far, everyone attended the annual Festival for Hermon.

~*~

Most every business was closed, no schools were in session, and anybody who was somebody was generally at the festival. It was an event for the entire family: faith, food, fun, games and other activities. Everything was always so wonderfully and festively decorated, with all sorts of aromatic fragrances filling the air. Fine linens draped all the buildings and overpasses. Hundreds filed into the clamoring streets for several days, everyone peaceably getting along, nothing but smiles and happiness.

It was also a time for relationships. Some who came were meeting for the first time, while others could renew or rekindle an old relationship. Everyone lived generally so far apart and spread out and was always too busy working and trying to earn a living that it left little time for any type of socialization ... except when there was a festival!

Some might not have seen each other since they were children, and as the years had grown, so had they. There were also a few springtime romances that managed to pop up. Perhaps from a chance glimpse or a smile, one's curiosity was peaked or just a mutual attraction was realized. Whatever the draw, people always had a good time at the festival.

The richest person
is not he
who has the most,
but he
who needs the least.
—Unknown

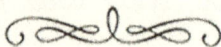

CLOSE

The men would all gather in one area and tell tall tales about their fishing or hunting adventures. The women would congregate to exchange recipes or just enjoy one another's company away from children. For their part, the children were free to run and play with little adult supervision and interruption. The young adults had their own space as well.

All throughout the city everyone seemed to be enjoying themselves ... except for one particular young girl who was sitting alone. She didn't appear to catch the interest of anyone, nor did anyone seem to interest her. She had traveled to the festival with her family, or so it was said. She didn't speak much, so no one knew her name. She was believed to have come from a small fishing village near Lake Tiberias, also known as the Sea of Galilee.

The whispers were that this young lady was from a noble family of Nunayya, the tower village, and her family had money. But, as I said earlier, she didn't talk all that much to anyone, so no one really knew her story for sure. She surely had lovely dark hair and beautiful dark eyes.

~*~

Perhaps it was those very same features that caught the eye of another loner in the crowd. This handsome young man was also very quiet and kept mostly to himself. His family was from another small village near the Galilee. His dad was a carpenter, and his mother was a stay-at-home mom, like so many other mothers were. The talk was that he helped his father with carpentry work from time to time, but he didn't want to go into the family woodworking business. He was more of an idealist type. He wanted to pursue something that would touch the lives of all people.

Some considered him to be just another idealist, someone who wanted to save the world. He was tall and quite firmly built, which might have been attributed to the type of work he did with his dad. Carpentry work was honest, hard work. Hauling the timbers, splitting the wood and sanding everything down to a smooth finish was not for the faint of heart. It required long hours of dedication. He was a blue collar guy from a working-class family, and the dark-haired girl was high society and supposedly from money. These two would never have met or perhaps even spoken outside of the festival. But it was festival time!

The young man felt a nudge to approach her. Out of all the people present that day, there was something about her that made her stand out from the crowd and caught his eye. It didn't seem to make sense, but he felt he had to try to speak with her.

He watched from a distance, as she carefully broke off crumbs of bread to feed some nearby birds. This seemed to him to indicate someone with a very kind heart, so he decided he would make his way through the dense crowd and across the street to the tree near where she was seated on a rock.

As the young man hid on the other side of the tree, out of sight of the young lady, he began to contemplate what he would say to a girl who had hardly spoken to anyone. He pondered several things in his head. What if they didn't speak the same language? After all, people came to the festival from all over. Would she look down upon him because of her wealth? Would she even acknowledge his presence? Finally, he decided to just give it a try, to see where everything would go.

He cleared his throat and stepped around the tree. Then, nothing! Nothing came out his mouth. He stood there with his mouth open in astonishment, looking at the bare rock that the dark-haired girl had once sat upon. She was gone! No girl! No birds! No bread!

His eyes quickly scanned up and down the streets, but he didn't see her anywhere. Had she run away after seeing him? Did she even see him? Did she know he was coming to talk with her? So many questions went through his mind. But he believed in destiny and knew that if they were supposed to meet, then one day they would. He shrugged his shoulders and thought to himself, "Perhaps another day." But he knew for sure he would never forget the dark-haired girl. In his heart, he believed he would see her again.

The heart sees what the eyes cannot

—Unknown

Hermon brought many people together throughout the years from all walks of life, and if these two were meant to be together, then it would surely happen, perhaps on another day.

Five Hundred Miles Away

As I mentioned earlier, Mount Hermon's reach was far and wide. It had been an iconic figure in this region dating back hundreds of years. If you've ever wondered where the Jordan River begins, the answer is right there at the snow-capped mountains that are visible from nearly everywhere in northern Israel. The mighty Jordan rises from the slopes of Mount Hermon, near the borders with Syria and Lebanon, before surfing south into the Sea of Galilee some sixty miles away. This is the highest point in the whole region. It has also long been known as a very mysterious place. There were quite a few tall tales told about this great mountain.

Urban legend has it that Hermon was once the land of Jurassic-age rocks, from the time of the dinosaurs. Some believed it was quite possible that those giant-sized reptiles could have roamed freely in that place. Could you picture seeing an eighteen-foot-tall herbivore like the Brachiosaurus munching on a shrub, or the largest and most powerful meat-eating predator, Tyrannosaurus Rex, looking you right in the eyes? If it were true, they weren't the only giants to have called Hermon home.

CLOSE

Not many places on earth can boast of the title "Secret Abode of the Gods." One such tale speaks of a great king who was two-thirds god and one-third man. According to the Epic of Gilgamesh, this king of Uruk built magnificent towers, surrounded his city with high walls and laid out orchards and fields. He was reported as being quite beautiful, immensely strong and extremely wise. He ruled with an iron fist over his kingdom and raped the women at his pleasure, all the while battling deities and monsters.

Leucothea, the Greek goddess of the sea, was also mentioned as having connections to Hermon, and the Nephilim, or Fallen Angels, are linked to this mysterious mountain as well. The Grigori, or "Watchers" as they were commonly known by many, were believed to have lived on the three summits of Mount Hermon because of its panoramic view of Heaven and Earth.

The Apocryphal book of Enoch states that Hermon was the place where two hundred rebellious angels fell to earth. These were creatures of great stature who towered over some of the tallest trees—if you believe the legend. They were said to have possessed immense strength, more than one hundred men combined, and had massive appetites.

Given that Hermon had lots of vegetation and wildlife, it made for the perfect location for a giant-size diet. The forest was crisscrossed with paths that

CLOSE

would take you all over the area, where you would find deer, fox, hedgehogs and many other tasty sources of protein. Some believed the giants to be heavenly beings who fell from the sky and came to dwell here on Earth but who desired to remain close to Heaven on the peaks of Hermon, perhaps hoping for a return one day.

I saw in the visions
of my head upon my bed,
and, behold, a watcher and an holy one
came down from heaven;

—Daniel 4:13[1]

1. The Holy Bible, English Standard Version, copyright © 2001 by Crossway Bibles.

These were the spiritual beings who observed and studied creation from the very beginning. But make no mistake, these were not gentle giants; nor did they display angelic personalities. On the contrary, they expressed very deviant behavior by terrorizing the nearby villages and abducting the women folk for their pleasure and procreation. In this way, they violated both their own nature and their appointed office. As you can imagine, these giants struck fear in the hearts of their neighbors.

The Nephilim reportedly survived the Great Flood, and their lineage was thought to be preserved in a race of giants that gave rise to the likes of the giant king of Bashan, a man named Og. His bed frame was said to have measured well over thirteen feet long and was more than six feet wide. His counterpart, the neighboring king of Heshbon, King Sihon, was said to be equal in size. The territory of these two great giant kings was the entire east side of Mount Hermon. There are many accounts told of their battles with the Israelites.

Another of their giant relatives was the now-infamous Philistine champion Goliath. Goliath, who was much smaller than his ancestors, only stood around ten feet tall and weighed in at a measly six hundred pounds. He had four brothers about his same size and stature. As a man dressed for battle, his sword was about five feet long and weighed more than twenty pounds. He was adorned in his bronze battle coat that weighed one hundred fifty pounds, while toting a twenty-six-foot-long javelin for long-range fighting. This human battle machine terrorized the Israeli army twice a day with death threats for several weeks until his demise at the hands of a small boy and his faithful slingshot.

In addition to its beauty and mystery, Hermon also served a utilitarian purpose as well. Remember, Hermon's footprint was quite large and covered more than five thousand acres, which made it one of the greatest geographical resources of the area. Its great height allowed it to capture an extreme amount of water in an otherwise normally dry area of the world, and that water nourished the region.

The mountain slopes of Hermon dropped straight down and extended into the middle of "The Golan" or Golan Heights. The Golan Heights had at least fifteen other mountains in its range and many of them were volcanic. All throughout this area, Hermon's presence could be felt as a vital source for plant life, vegetation, various types of vineyards and several trees species of oak, pine and poplar.

Several communities and villages also benefited from Hermon's water flowing into the Sea of Galilee then on to the River Jordan, places like Caesarea Philippi, located at its base, the city of Tyre on the banks of the Mediterranean, Bethsaida, Capernaum, Magdala, Cana, Nazareth and even as far down as Jerusalem itself. In fact, many villages sprang up just because of the Sea of Galilee and the enormous fishing industry it supported.

The Sea of Galilee, which covered some sixty-four square miles and, at its deepest part, was more than one hundred and fifty feet deep, was believed to be home to at least twenty-four different species of fish. This grand area would impact the entire world!

To whom much is given

Much will be given.

— Benton T. Thompson, III

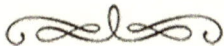

Four Hundred Miles Away

One village that benefited greatly from the freshwater fish that the Sea of Galilee offered up was Nunayya, also known as Magdala Nunayya, which means "fish tower." Magdala Nunayya, or simply Magdala, was blessed to have land with lots of natural salt mines around it. This soon became a great asset in the fishing industry. Given that all the fish caught in the immediate area were freshwater fish, they wouldn't last very long before needing to be eaten. This limited buyers to only those who could consume the catch right away. But there was a family in Magdala that realized very quickly how to capitalize on the abundance of salt and fish. A man by the name of Cyrus, along with his wife Eucharis and their three children—Martha, Mary and Lazarus—figured out pretty quickly that salted fish would last considerably longer. Through the process of salting the catch, they were able to preserve it for days, not just minutes.

Cyrus and his family built a tiny building to store the salt they gathered from the local salt mines. When the fishermen brought in the fish, they would pack them in salt, thus ensuring that the fish would last for several days longer than usual. Business boomed as more fishermen heard of the salting process which would allow them to sell more fish to more people. The days and hours of operation grew longer and longer as the word got out.

Things began going so well that the tiny building Cyrus had built would no longer meet the demand. So, he had a huge tower constructed, much like a large silo to store the salt. This became known as the Fish Salting Tower and, hence, the town got its name—Magdala Nunayya, the "fish tower."

In time, Cyrus and his family became very wealthy as a result of their business venture. They had not been privileged, but had come into their money in a short period of time. As with anyone who is suddenly thrust into a new situation, it is understandable to think that there would be an adjustment period. Each of the members of the family had to learn to cope with their newfound success and stature in the community in their own way.

For the parents, the adjustment was not necessarily as challenging as it was for the three children. Martha, being the eldest, had always been very level-headed and conservative, even from a small child. She was a practical person by nature, the responsible one, you might say. So no real riffs could be seen in her personality, except that she became a compulsive organizer. Everything had a place, and it needed to be in its place. Maybe this was due to having more things to organize.

Mary, the middle child, was a bit more whimsical and explorative. She leaned more toward the non-conformist side of the scales. As a middle child, she felt stuck in between the perfect Daddy's girl, Martha, and Lazarus, the Baby of the bunch, who could do no wrong, even if he were to have burned the house down.

The result was that Mary often sought the attention she wanted from her father from others, and because of it, she was often judged by others as a woman of low morals or of ill repute.

As for Lazarus, he was just a kind soul who never harmed anyone. He was the passive one in the family. While others might have made a fuss over him, he simply downplayed it all. Lazarus wanted no special attention; he just wanted to be a regular guy.

Growing up as working heirs to the father's estate didn't leave any of them with much time for personal relationships, but they certainly had each other. Since Mary was a little more outgoing than the rest, things began happening so quickly that she barely knew what to think of it.

CLOSE

Mary was a very attractive girl with lovely dark hair and beautiful dark eyes. She would often withdraw into herself out of concern, wondering if people only wanted to be her friend because they knew her family had money and some nobility. She loved to retreat into the foothills of Hermon, just to smell the Lavender Mountain Lily that always had a very calming effect on whatever was happening in her life at the time. She would often take long walks along the pathways and hillsides. Hermon gave her so many good memories.

Mary recalled, as a young girl, attending a festival for Hermon in Jerusalem. What a beautiful spectacle that had been! All the food, fragrances, colors, flowers and people! But that adventure had been short-lived because she didn't really meet anyone new there. She did recall seeing one boy who hid behind a tree near where she was sitting, but she had gotten so "creeped out" by it that she got up and left.

"Oh well, perhaps another day," Mary recalled thinking. She wondered what he wanted. What would he have said? "If it were meant to be, then it will be," she concluded. All things considered, Mary and her siblings were pretty good people at their core.

Let parents bequeath
to their children not riches,
but the spirit of reverence.

—Plato

5

Three Hundred Miles Away

While Magdala Nunayya was becoming more popular, there was also another community along the shores of the Sea of Galilee that was growing in notoriety as well. It was a little town called Bethsaida on the northeast shoreline at the place where the Jordan River merged into the Sea of Galilee. Bethsaida, which means "house of the fishermen," was a thriving fishing town, as its name suggests. Some of its most notable citizens were fishermen. Among those fishermen with such recognition were men like Philip, Peter and Andrew.

Peter and his brother, Andrew, loved to fish, and they were always out early every morning, even after having spent full nights out fishing on the lake. Neither of them was going to get rich fishing, but they loved it nonetheless. The buzz around Bethsaida had less to do with the fishermen and more to do with a young preacher (or Rabbi, as he was called by some) who had recently come into their midst. Little did the two brothers know that they would soon have their own personal encounter with the new preacher.

CLOSE

One day, after a long night of fishing with very little to show for it, the brothers decided to call it quits. The plan was to just head home and give it a go the next night—just as they had done the night before and the night before that. However, this time was different. They didn't realize that someone had been watching them very intently from on shore.

On the final throw for the day, Andrew took the huge net with the weights on all ends and whirled it around over his head, round and round several times. Then he flung it out over the water and allowed it to sink to the bottom. Once it had disappeared from the surface and gone down several feet, it would be his brother's turn to get involved. Peter would begin pulling on the rope, to gather the net, while drawing it to the surface to see what they might have caught. This was the pattern they had already repeated several times earlier. As they pulled in yet another empty net, like they had several times throughout the night, they were interrupted by a sound. The onlooker who had been watching them was now calling to them.

As I stated earlier, Peter and Andrew loved to fish, so it didn't matter to them so much whether they caught a lot or a little, as long as they were fishing. Now they heard a voice calling from the bank, "Hello, fishermen!"

CLOSE

They looked up to see someone waving and motioning to them. He was calling out, "Cast your nets in the other direction, and you will receive a great harvest."

"Who is this guy?" they thought to themselves. He's not dressed like a fisherman, and they didn't recognize him from the area.

Peter, being the eldest, spoke up and said, "Sir, we fish this lake all the time. No one ever catches anything much this time of day. Thank you kindly for the advice, but we are finished for now."

The stranger shouted back, "Then surely one more cast in that direction over there couldn't possibly hurt anything."

By this time, others were gathering around the spectacle on the lake. So the fishermen decided to oblige the onlooker and cast their nets one more time, in the direction he had pointed. When they did, they were utterly amazed. It was a miracle. When they pulled the net up this time, it was overflowing with fish. The two brothers laughed with excitement over this incredible event.

After getting the fish safely into the boat, the two quickly rowed toward the shore, where the stranger who had just amazed them was still standing. They just had to see who this man was who knew more about fishing on the Galilee than they did.

CLOSE

As they got closer, they saw that it was a young man they didn't recognize from anywhere around. As their boat neared the shore, he began to speak.

There is no limit
to how many times
you can go fishing.
—Unknown

The young stranger said, "How would you two like a challenge of a different sort?"

Peter said, "What type of challenge? We're just simple fishermen."

The stranger said, "How would you like to hook the hearts of men and help them change their lives for the better?"

Peter answered, "That sounds like an interesting challenge, but, like I said, we're just simple fishermen, not eloquent speakers."

The stranger surprised them by saying that they were exactly the type of people he was looking for. "Just as you two trusted me today and got a great catch, we shall do the same together as we trust each other," he said. "Will you trust me yet further?"

When the brothers nodded their heads in agreement to what he had said, he continued, "Well, then, pull your boat ashore and follow me."

CLOSE

By this time, even more onlookers had gathered to see the bounty that had been caught. Motioning to the fish, Peter said to the man, "What of our fish?"

"Leave them for the others," was the surprising answer, "it will surely be a blessing to their families." So off they went, walking and talking together like old friends who had recently reunited.

"I am a new preacher in town," the man said, "and I'm traveling all throughout the area sharing a message of hope. My plan is to reignite the hearts of men through faith."

"But why did you select us?" Andrew questioned. "We're not preachers."

"Well, fishing is very similar to what I intend to accomplish," the stranger said.

"Let me explain it a bit more. The work you do as fishermen is honest hard work, and so, too, is what I do. You endure daily hardships, trials and unexpected challenges, and it requires dedication and perseverance because you don't know where your next catch will come from.

"Ministry requires that same commitment. Human souls are the fish, the world is the sea, the message is the net by which we shall gather them, and eternal life is the shore we seek to take them to. So, you see, you already have the skillset that is needed for the work to be done. You were already qualified. All I did was call you. I can only call those who have already been pre-qualified."

CLOSE

Peter and Andrew thought this was a very peculiar statement, but, for the moment, they just filed it away in their hearts.

~*~

As they walked and talked, the young preacher began to share how he felt, that one's faith should be an essential part of their life. He spoke of his own faith in God and how it was at the very center of everything he believed and did. He told them that having faith in someone is based upon the relationship that you have with that person. The more reliable you felt that person was, the greater the faith you could have in them.

The two brothers listened intently as he spoke, and he gave them an example from their own experiences. "Every day you go and jump into the boat to begin fishing, without knowing if there is a leak in the hull. That's faith!" he said. "You sit down on a chair, not knowing if it can even support your weight. That's faith!" As they walked on, he offered countless other examples in which they had displayed faith in things in daily life without knowing or understanding how they worked.

Up ahead of them, there were three other fishermen working on their nets, getting ready to leave for home. Seeing them, the young preacher said, "Fishermen, may I speak with you before you leave?"

It was a father and his two sons, and they agreed to hear him out. He shared the same message with them that he had with Peter and Andrew. "Join me," he said to them, "and let's fish for the souls of men."

Andrew and Peter chimed in and told of their recruitment as well. That was enough for the two brothers, James and John, to say goodbye to their father Zebedee and follow the preacher as well.

6

Two Hundred Miles Away

This was the start of the young preacher's ministry, and it proved to be a good one. His following and fame began to spread all throughout the community and region. He was soon known all around the Galilee, and as far away as Jerusalem and beyond.

The mystique of this young, dynamic and unconventional teacher also caught the eye (and the ire) of the very traditional church elders in the community. He performed many amazing feats that no one had ever seen before. The elders, being like so many others, sought to discredit that which they could not easily explain or understand. Some went so far as to say that the man was practicing witchcraft and casting spells on the people. Others said he worshiped the devil by offering ritual sacrifices. There were those who said that he was nothing more than a lowly trickster who had set out to deceive innocent and unintelligent people. As his following grew to having twelve companion ministers and seventy deacons, so, too, did the criticism of him, his techniques and his abilities.

CLOSE

Terrible things were spoken about the man and his family. This was hard to understand since he was a man who sought to reignite the faith of those who were said to already be faithful. He had people being healed from blindness, sickness, lameness and demonic spirits. He caused thousands to be fed by very little means on various occasions. Miracles happened everywhere he went. This activity made some love him, but it made others revile him.

Some looked upon this preacher as just a sideshow carnival act, but that didn't seem to matter to him. His message and his purpose remained constant throughout it all—to ignite faith within the hearts of men! His assignment was not to be as God, but rather to be as a man who would lead people to God. He loved God and wanted to show others how to love God too.

<hr>

And the Word (Christ) became flesh,

and lived among us;

and we [actually] saw His glory

—John 1:14[2]

<hr>

The young preacher had one purpose for his ministry, and that was to show people how to have faith in God. "If you will dare to have faith," he said,

---

2. The Amplified Bible, copyright © 2015 by The Lockman Foundation, La Habra, CA 90631. All rights reserved.

"then anything is possible to you."

One definition of faith is "having complete confidence or trust in someone," and he had complete confidence and trust in God. He trusted Him explicitly, and he desired for everyone else to do the same.

Much of this trust had been groomed during his alone time with God on long walks on the slopes of Mount Hermon. There he could clear his head and just relax among nature. Observing the deer enjoying the cool water made him reflect on what David had said, "Like a deer pants for streams of water, so my soul pants for You."

He watched the sparrow fluttering about with no concerns and remembered the word of the Lord that said He would not allow one sparrow to fall to the ground.

Noticing a thrush preparing itself for migration, he recalled the Word of God that said, "Your heavenly Father feeds them, and you are even more valuable."

All these things spoke of having trust and faith in God. God even cared for the creatures of nature, so how much more must He care for men and women? Experiences like these often gave the young preacher homilies that he would share with others. Once he gave a teaching on faith using a tiny mustard seed as an example of what a small amount of faith in God could do. In this way, he pointed out that with God nothing is impossible.

There were many times when he would recognize someone for their faith and how their faith had healed them. In one story, there was a woman who had been hemorrhaging for twelve years. She came up behind him and touched the hem of his clothes and was immediately healed. He said to her, "Take heart, daughter. Your faith has healed you." Her long-time flow of blood had ceased.

On another occasion, he shared with his minister companions that they had displayed a lack of faith, and, therefore, nothing had happened. Faith was the key.

~*~

Once they were all on a boat crossing the lake when a terrible storm arose. The young preacher was resting in the boat because he was tired. The storm frightened the others so badly that they woke him up, asking him to get up and do something. They could see that he was not afraid. He had faith that God would not allow anything to happen to them, so he spoke to the storm to be at peace, and, amazingly, it obeyed him.

When this happened, the young preacher asked his companions, "Why are you so afraid? Do you still have NO faith?" He implored them to have faith, a complete trust and confidence in God, that all things are possible when you believe or trust in Him.

Everywhere the man went and to everyone he spoke to, it was regarding his faith and how they could have the same kind of faith. The young preacher taught faith, not chance, and "there is a distinct difference between the two," he insisted. "Faith has to do with your 'complete confidence and trust in the ability of someone to do something,' while chance is 'an optimistic attitude in one's state of mind based on an expectation rooted in desire.' Faith believes and expects it to happen, while chance looks for it to possibly, maybe happen sometime in the future ... if the stars align.

"Chance is rather like a gamble, but

God is a sure thing, not a gamble in any sense of the word. Having faith in the love and sovereignty of God is arguably the most prevalent concept all throughout the Bible."

Many of those he spoke to were familiar with the stories of Moses having faith in God at the opening of the Red Sea, when the Pharaoh was chasing him, or Joshua, believing God for the sun and time to stand still while he defeated an enemy of His people. Certainly they had heard Abraham's story of having a child when he was more than a hundred years old and his wife was in her nineties. Their miracle happened because they believed God when He promised them a son.

CLOSE

The young preacher taught this same concept of having faith in God to anyone who would listen, and his message was reiterated over and over again everywhere he went.

Not everyone was enthusiastic about the idea that their faith needed to be reignited. One example of a place where the message was not received was a small village about two miles from Capernaum that sat upon a hill just north of the Sea of Galilee. It was called Chorazin. In fact, not only Chorazin, but also Bethsaida, where three of his disciples were from, and Capernaum all experienced some great miracles, and yet they rejected his message of faith in God.

Then he began to reproach the cities

in which most of his deeds

of power had been done,

because they did not repent.

"Woe to you, Chorazin!

Woe to you, Bethsaida!

And you, Capernaum,

will you be exalted to heaven?

No, you will be brought

down to Hades.

—Matthew 11:21-22[3]

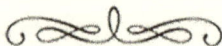

3. Holy Bible, New International Version, copyright ©1973, 1978, 1984, 2011 by Biblica, Inc.

7

One Hundred Miles Away

Except for a few areas that reacted negatively to him, the young preacher saw many more who did receive his message of faith in God. In a place called Cana, a nobleman believed, and his son was healed. Then, at a wedding, the preacher provided a great surprise for the happy couple and their guests, and many believed in that place.

In Capernaum, he helped Peter's mother-in-law overcome a deadly fever, a paralytic fully recovered, a man with a withered hand was healed, and two blind men received their sight. Galileans also experienced lepers being cured.

At Gennesaret, there was a multitude of more than five thousand who had a faith-infused meal from a small boy's lunch. The word was certainly getting out about the power of faith through this man and the miracles he did.

The young preacher and his disciples walked the entire region, igniting the hearts of men. He had certain routes and pathways that he preferred to use from one place to another. Wadi Hamam, for instance, was a pathway that he regularly used to travel from his hometown of Nazareth, across the mountainside of Hermon and into the Upper Galilee. This path led into his new home village of Capernaum, where Peter, Andrew, James and John lived, as well as Matthew, another disciple, a tax collector.

The young preacher would also frequently walk to Sepphoris where his mother had been born and onward to Cana, then eastward to the Sea of Galilee, where the valley of the lake's shore flowed into that booming fishing town called Magdala. Capernaum, where he lived, was also in northern Galilee, a short distance from Magdala, along the shore of the sea.

During his journeys southward into Jerusalem, he would often go by way of the northwest shore of the Sea of Galilee through Magdala, and there he would pass that huge tower, the place where the fish were salted and sold.

A synagogue stood in the center of the town as a reminder of the people's commitment to fellowship with the only Source of all life, the One True and Living God.

~*~

Cyrus and his family had been instrumental in the erection of both of these facilities. Aside from the fish salting, the village was best known for boat building. It was perfectly positioned at the shore of the Sea of Galilee and at the mouth of the valley that ascended to Upper Galilee, and further to the ports of the Mediterranean as well as sitting at the junction of an important Roman road that led from Lower Galilee to Damascus.

Magdala was able to export products to markets everywhere from this location. This village was a special place to the people in the community, as well as to the young preacher.

By this time, the fame of him and the miracles he was involved with had spread all throughout the land.

Quite often, large crowds would gather around to hear him speak. Once, as he was walking along the Sea of Galilee, many in need began to gather around him, having heard of the miracles he commanded. He retreated upward to higher ground so as to see everyone, and took a seat on a huge overhanging rock.

As he began to speak, the people grew in faith, and those who were ill, lame and troubled stepped up to receive healing. He ministered to them for hours on end. Great crowds continued to come and lay the mute, the crippled and blind before him to be healed.

One day the hour grew late, and he, nor his disciples, nor the crowd had eaten a thing. His heart was touched with compassion for them to have something to eat before they left. He inquired of his disciples just how much food they had. Their answer was swift and resolute, "Not enough to feed this crowd of four thousand or so people!"

The young preacher told them to bring him what they had. They brought him seven loaves of bread and a few small fish. He smiled and had everyone sit down in reverence to God. Then he began praying and exalting God for His greatness and goodness toward them, recalling many of the blessings that He had blessed them with, all the times that God had not let them down. He said he knew this time would be no different.

Next, he expressed his desire to supply the people's natural hunger just as their spiritual hunger had been satisfied, because of their faith in God. He concluded by thanking God for always providing everything they needed.

After praying, he told the disciples to hand out the food. Amazingly, everyone received plenty to eat, and there were lots of leftovers. It was a miracle. This was a prime example of the young preacher praying a prayer of faith to God, believing that He would supply their needs and a miracle happened.

Life is a series of thousands

of tiny little miracles.

Notice them.

—Unknown

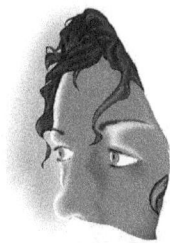

Seventy-Five Miles Away

The young preacher sent the crowd away and got into a boat with some of his disciples to retreat to the other side of the lake toward Magdala. When they reached the shore, he told them he would meet them at the little synagogue in town after he took a walk. He set out walking and talking to God as he often did in his times of solitude. He paused to sit on a rock and continued to thank God for

His goodness toward him, and he heard a noise behind him, the crackle of a branch on the ground. Perhaps it was an animal out for an evening stroll. As the sounds persisted and got closer, he called out, "Hello! Is anyone there? Hello!"

A voice responded. Then, stepping through the trees, a dark figure stood just to the side of where he was seated. "I'm sorry if I disturbed you," the voice from the shadows said. "It was not my intentions to do so. I was merely out taking a walk in this beautiful moonlight."

He smiled and said, "I, too, was enjoying the moonlight."

"Again, I apologize, and I will continue my walk and let you do likewise," the voice said.

CLOSE

The young preacher asked, "Who are you? And where are you from?"

Then, as the figure stepped out into the light, he could see that it was a woman. She said, "My name is Mary, and I am from Magdala."

"I am the new preacher," he said, "please come and sit with me. The moon is big enough for both of us to share its beauty."

Mary did as requested, and they began by sharing the things they both loved about Mount Hermon, most importantly the Lavender Mountain Lilys. On and on they went for hours just sharing stories of their lives.

Mary mentioned to him that she had heard of the young teacher who performed miracles and that she, too, was in need of a miracle. She went on to tell him how she and her family had been instrumental in building the synagogue and how they had begun the family business of salting the fish.

The young preacher shared that he was on his way to meet his disciples at that very synagogue and invited her to join him. She consented.

While walking, they continued conversing like two old friends. There was a certain familiarity about their speech toward one another.

Eventually, Mary shared how, years earlier, she had attended a festival in Jerusalem. He smiled and said, "Mary, the Magdalene ... that's where I saw you for the very first time. You were the beautiful, dark-haired, dark-eyed girl I saw sitting on a rock feeding the birds. I was coming to approach you, but you left."

Mary, or the Magdalene, as she was so often called, said she hadn't known what to expect. "I noticed you peering at me from across the street. Then I saw you cross over and hide behind a tree. It seemed like you were there for quite a while."

The young preacher laughed and said, "I was just trying to get up the nerve to speak to you."

Mary continued, "I didn't know what you were planning, so I thought I'd better get out of there before something happened to me."

The two laughed and laughed as they reminisced on that brief encounter. Now, at the base of Mount Hermon, in the twilight hours of evening, although many years had since passed, these two were finally able to meet. "Some day" had finally come. It was a very heart-warming experience for the both of them.

~*~

When Mary and the preacher reached the synagogue, the disciples asked him who his traveling companion was. "This is Mary, the Magdalene," he said. "She needs my help, and I will help her."

CLOSE

Mary described instances in which she had experienced memory loss, times when she could no longer recall personal events in her life. She also shared about other times of abuse, depression, rage and hostility. She detailed a life that experienced various challenges that had left her at times not really knowing who she was.

The young preacher began praying for her, thanking God for being faithful to keep her through it all, always being there with her and bringing her safely to this moment when He would cleanse her from her past, restore her and make her a new person. Mary wept as he prayed that beautiful prayer.

The young preacher kept giving God praise for Mary's life. After he ended the prayer, he embraced the Magdalene and told her to go now and begin her new life free of the chains of the past.

Mary, because she was very wealthy and very beautiful, had once used those traits to indulge in carnal pleasures. As a result, she had lost her good name and had been simply referred to as "a sinner." But God had, once again, shown her great grace and made know His love for her, and she was now fully restored.

At that moment, Mary vowed never to forget what God had done for her, and the young preacher assured her that they would definitely see one another again.

CLOSE

Tell me and I forget.
Teach me and I remember.
Involve me and I learn.

—Benjamin Franklin

The young preacher and his disciples continued on to help all who were willing to increase their faith. He kept his messages very simple and direct, often teaching using parables to illustrate his point so that others could get a visual of the truth he was speaking about. There were those in the crowd who would leave remembering the parable or story he had shared. A few would leave committed with an understanding of how to apply the message they had heard to their daily life. Others left uncommitted but later, through reflection, realized the intent of the message and had a life change. Sadly, many left not hearing, not receiving, not accepting and not being willing to make any lifestyle change at all.

Generally, the more intimate the setting the greater the detail was in the sharing. When there were large crowds, the preacher usually preferred to teach in parables. A parable shared the truth in a hidden message, and only those who were willing to dig for the answer would find it.

As an example, one day the young preacher left his home in Capernaum and began walking along the shore of the Galilee with his disciples. As he walked, he pointed out to them how some birds were circling above them overhead. He noticed how they would fly by and then swoop down on the hillside.

Large crowds began to gather around to see him, so he used a nearby boat to launch out into the Sea of Galilee to address the people who stood on the shoreline. The young preacher began by turning the attention of the crowd toward the birds which were flying overhead, making them aware of how they were swooping down on the hilly terrain of Galilee. He also had them notice the exposed black basalt rocks that were scattered all around. Farmers had to clear all those rocks away before planting their seeds. Otherwise, as he pointed out to them, when the farmer or sower began to sow his seeds, some would fall on rocky ground and eventually die because the soil wasn't deep enough to allow for growth.

The young preacher knew that many among them were farmers. He told them to notice how many birds came to the area in their migration and would swarm the fields as the farmers began their planting. If a farmer became distracted, trying to shoo the many birds away from his newly-planted fields, he would inadvertently sling some seed on the roadside. This worked perfectly into the plan of the birds, that would quickly swoop in and eat them up.

This distraction caused some seeds not to receive deliberate and directed sowing. Their sowing was random, without intent or purpose. And, without enough soil to allow them to find cover and, thus, go unnoticed, as well as without receiving proper nourishment through watering, that seed was destined for failure when the dry season came.

"There will always be a dry season in the future," he said. He never spoke in vague terms, but illustrated a vision that was both familiar and relevant to most in the region.

One day he shared this parable with the crowd:

"*Listen! Behold, a sower went out to sow.*
And as he sowed,
some seed fell along the path,
and the birds came and devoured it.
Other seed fell on rocky ground,
where it did not have much soil,
and immediately it sprang up,
since it had no depth of soil.
And when the sun rose, it was scorched,
and since it had no root,
it withered away.
Other seed fell among thorns,
and the thorns grew up and choked it,
and it yielded no grain.

CLOSE

And other seeds fell into good soil

and produced grain,

growing up and increasing

and yielding thirtyfold

and sixtyfold

and a hundredfold."

And he said, "He who has ears to hear,

let him hear."

—Mark 4:3-8[4]

He later shared with his disciples the meaning of the parable: "The seed is the Word of the Kingdom of God," he said. "The various soil types represent a person's heart toward God. They were four different examples of how a

---

4. The Holy Bible, English Standard Version, copyright © 2001 by Crossway Bibles.

human heart responds to the Word of God." He shared this to draw them Close. He was preparing them for the days ahead.

~9~

Fifty Miles Away

After the young preacher had spoken these things, he began to move away from that place. As he and the disciples were walking, they were approached by the Magdalene and two other women. The Magdalene shared with the young preacher that she had heard his message, and her heart was very receptive to the Word of God. She expressed her desire to be close to him. She told him that she believed in the work he was doing and, being a first-hand recipient of the grace of God, she felt that she owed it to the Lord to help support his ministry and become one of his trusted disciples. She ended by saying that she would be forever grateful to him for all he had done for her.

This was a rare event, given that previously no one whom the young preacher had healed had ever made the decision to become a follower of his, not those with blinded eyes who now saw, not the lame who now walked, and not the sick who were now healed. Not one previous recipient of the grace of God had been willing to dedicate their life to the Lord in service.

CLOSE

There was one occasion when the young preacher and his disciples were walking down a road and several people were following behind them. One man in the crowd said to him, "I will follow you wherever you go." But when the young preacher responded that he was, in effect, homeless and had no place to lay his head, the man disappeared and was never seen again.

On another occasion, he asked a group of people in the crowd, "Will you follow me?" One man's response was that he couldn't right then because he had to go home and bury his father. Another said, "Lord, I will follow you right after I go home and speak with my family." But the Magdalene was different; she was special. Not only did she make the decision to follow the young preacher; she also brought along two other women as fellow recruits.

The three of them were not your average citizens. As I have said, the Magdalene was a beautiful and wealthy woman who had been judged by society as "fallen." Once even described as "mentally ill," now she was healed and restored.

She was joined by her friend Joanna, who was the wife of one of the chief stewards of King Herod. Herod himself was a very outspoken opponent of this ministry. In fact, the king had sought to kill the young preacher soon after his birth. None of this mattered to Joanna. She, too, had great prestige and wealth, but she was willing to risk it all to follow the young preacher and the truth of his message.

Then there was Susannah, whose name means "lily." She came from a family of means as well. Susannah had been searching for real truth all her life, and now she had found it. That bond of truth is what had brought Mary and her friends together in the first place, and now together they could follow the Truth.

For a time, these three women provided most of the financial support for the ministry out of their own monies, as well as through some fundraising efforts they did along the way. They also helped with domestic support by washing and mending clothes, cooking food, running errands and, in many other ways, making themselves available to assist wherever there was a need.

Some people attached a social stigma to the women because they traveled with a group of men, something that was unheard of in those days. But the Magdalene and the other women did not let this get in the way of them following the young preacher. As he went throughout every village and city, preaching and teaching the glad tidings of the Kingdom of God, they followed and assisted him. His disciples were both men and women. This sent a powerful message to all people, that this ministry was inclusive of all believers.

~*~

The young preacher continued to regularly get his alone time, although sometimes he would invite one or two of his disciples to join him. The Magdalene was very often present at his side. During his times of solitude, he went deeper in his love relationship with God, whom he knew as Abba. Sometimes he would spend all night praying and communicating with his Father.

Benton T. Thompson, III

＊＊＊

One of those days Jesus
went out to a mountainside
to pray, and spent the night
praying to God.
—Luke 6:12[5]

＊＊＊

This was a scene that became very familiar over the years of the young preacher's ministry. Time and time again the disciples saw him consistently anchor himself in God's presence through prayer. He was not only a savior, but also a friend, mentor and teacher to all who followed him. They saw him face

5. Holy Bible, New International Version, copyright ©1973, 1978, 1984, 2011 by Biblica, Inc

almost every situation imaginable. They watched as he regularly avoided the spotlight and the accolades of men. He let his followers know that God alone was the single focal point of his lie and ministry, and he would never give into any self-ambitions or self-promotions.

The young preacher led by example. His goal for these men and women closest to him was to teach them discipline in all areas of their life. His challenge was to correct how they thought and perceived situations. He used real-life moments and mistakes as opportunities to reveal to them greater truths about the inner workings of the Kingdom of God.

Some disciples had family and other responsibilities to tend to, so he would call them all together from time to time to ensure that they all received certain teachings.

The ministry purpose of the apostles of the young preacher was two-fold: 1). They were to preach the good news that the Kingdom of God had come and was now available to everyone, and 2). They were to heal the sick among them. This was done to show the connection between the spiritual and the natural realm.

There was a lot of diversity in the original group of disciples. A third of them were common fishermen, not very well educated, but hard workers nonetheless. One was considered to be a thief and traitor because of his profession as a tax collector. Another was a rebel rouser, constantly set on overthrowing the government. Each had their own path to the Lord. This group formed an inner circle of apostles.

There were a few who seemed to want to hear and know more. Prominent among them were Peter, Andrew, James and John. In addition to these four, the Magdalene was constantly at the young preacher's side, listening, learning and willing to serve him whenever possible. He also got to know and love each of their families as well.

He truly loved the Magdalene's little brother Lazarus because of his youthful zeal for life. He appreciated how her sister Martha was always willing to pitch in wherever needed.

Peter was well versed in both the Jewish and Greek culture. He was a devout family man, and he took his wife with him when he visited various churches and gatherings of believers. He and his in-laws shared a home together.

The young preacher loved the fact that Peter was a family man. Therefore, Peter would often assume the role of spokesperson for the group. He was the first among them to move, the first to volunteer and, unfortunately, also the first to lose heart at times.

And then there was Peter's brother Andrew. Andrew was happy to remain in the background. He was not nearly as outspoken as his brother Peter, but he played a significant role nonetheless. Andrew was more personable, so he wanted to get to know the young preacher better on a personal level. He wanted everyone to have a personal relationship with him. That is certainly a trait that put him in the inner circle.

Then we have the sons of Zebedee, James and John, otherwise known as the Sons of Thunder because of their fiery temperament. John had first been a follower of John the Baptist, another fiery preacher. (Interestingly enough, John was the cousin of the young preacher.) James and John were brimming with overconfidence. It would appear that they got it naturally, since their mother, Mary Salome, asked the young preacher if one of her sons could share the throne with him when he came into his kingdom. She didn't fully realize that her request meant a cruel and heartless death for the chosen candidate. Still, Mary Salome and her two sons were always a part of the inner circle. Mary Salome had another connection to the young preacher; she was his mother's half-sister.

The preacher experienced the brothers' temperament on a number of occasions, like the time they asked to call fire down on a Samaritan village. Although

CLOSE

they were sometimes intolerant and self-seeking, they were very passionate about their love for the young preacher. That was never questioned. And, because of their great love for him, he drew them (and their mother) even closer.

❧

The language of friendship is not words, but meanings!
—Henry David Thoreau

❧

The Magdalene, Peter, Andrew, James and John were privileged to be with the young preacher when he healed the daughter of Jairus, the ruler of the synagogue and many other miracles. He loved all the disciples and their families, but some remained especially close to him.

~10~

Twenty-Five Miles Away

The young preacher was careful to give all of his followers specific instructions about their ministry and message. They were all to go from village to village sharing the message of faith in God. He wanted them equipped only with the Gospel, nothing else. They had to trust that God would provide their needs—even their food, water and shelter. This would increase their faith, as well as their ability to share with others how to believe.

What a great testimony this would provide! If they were to have a roof over their heads at night and food on the table, the power of God would have to be real in and through them to make it happen. The Gospel they were preaching would have to work for them first. If they didn't work God's Word, then God's Word wouldn't work for them. No work, no eat!

Had they been allowed to take along all the necessities, their faith would not have grown nearly as much. The lesson was not how much do you know "of" God, but rather how much do you trust "in" God. This was in direct contrast to the teachings of many in the traditional church. These disciples would have to live and walk by faith, for the young preacher was teaching them to trust God by having them do that which was beyond their means.

Just as the male disciples were learning to hone and polish their ministry gifts, so, too, was the Magdalene. Her perspective on the Gospel was more unique than any of her brother apostles, not because she was a woman (although that did help to shape her ministry some), but, rather, because she was personally a miracle of the grace of God. Because God had healed her person, she became a living testimony to His power.

Mary didn't often speak about her past, at least around the other disciples. She did speak about it when she was ministering to those who had a similar history. She would readily share her testimony of how she had been far from God, and yet His grace and mercy had brought her close to Him. She told of a time when she had prostituted her body, engaging in all manner of despicable behavior and had actually been on the verge of taking her own life. Then, one day, she had heard of the young preacher and his message of God's great love—even for those who had fallen.

CLOSE

Mary would go on to tell how she had dared to believe that God could somehow still love her.

⧫

You, LORD,
brought me up
from the realm of the dead;
You spared me from
going down to the pit.
—Psalm 30:3[6]

⧫

When Mary had met the young preacher, he had embodied the love of God. He didn't condemn or judge her for her past Instead, he gave her

6. Holy Bible, New International Version, copyright ©1973, 1978, 1984, 2011 by Biblica, Inc

hope. He showed her love, God's love. And, through his intervention, God had given her beauty for ashes. She no longer needed to hide in the shadows of shame about her past; she could now walk in the sunshine of God's restoration and encourage and help others to do the same. Many women, as well as men, had very similar experiences to Mary's, and so her words, her message, her very life healed a great many who, like her, had once been broken.

The young preacher was very proud of Mary's faith and ministry. In fact, her ministry even touched his own mother's life. She was also named Mary, and there were things in her heart that she felt free to share with the Magdalene. The two would spend countless hours together fellowshipping and sharing about the goodness of God, the wonders they had seen and the miracles they had experienced.

Mary liked having the Magdalene around; the two of them genuinely liked one another. The young preacher would sometimes be there too, enjoying the company of two women he loved dearly. Moments like those and the ones he spent at Hermon were some of the young preacher's most precious times.

Mary, his mother, and the Magdalene both knew that he enjoyed his times of prayer and solitude away on Mount Hermon, and that was why they both had the Mountain Lavender Lily growing in pots around their homes. The smell of the wild lavender was very soothing and relaxing. They did this so that he could have a place of peace, a respite from the challenges of his daily ministry.

At one point, the group traveled again to Jerusalem. After they had arrived and while the young preacher was resting, the Magdalene took the opportunity to go visit her brother and sister, whom she had not seen in a while. They were now staying in their house in Bethany, not so far away.

When the Magdalene reached their home, she found Martha lamenting over the fact that Lazarus had been sickly for a few days. They sent someone to tell the young preacher about this and to ask him to come as soon as he could. He was back out ministering wherever he could find a willing heart, and when word of this sickness finally reached him, he was ministering in a far village. As soon as he had finished the ministry, the group began the long trek to Bethany to see what could be done for Lazarus.

By the time they reached the home of their friends in Bethany, the Magdalene and her sister Martha greeted him with tears. "You're too late!" Martha said through her sobs. "Lazarus is dead."

The young preacher began to cry too. Then he said, "Where is his body? Take me to him!"

Both women insisted that their brother had been dead for quite some time now and that his body was already prepared for burial. "He smells of rotting flesh," they said, "and he's already in his tomb."

The young preacher looked into the eyes of the Magdalene and asked her if she trusted him. With tears in her eyes, she nodded her head up and down, to indicate yes. He asked Martha the same thing. He told them both that if they trusted him, they would see the greatness of God's love and glory that very day. Then, again, he said, "Take me to his body." And, as they walked, he was praying.

Once they reached the place where Lazarus' body lay, the young preacher began to thank God out loud for the miracle He was about to perform. He said it loud enough for everyone to hear. He then spoke directly to the dead and commanded Lazarus to come up and out of the tomb.

For a moment, there was only a deafening silence. Nothing happened. A large crowd had gathered by this time, having heard of the death of Lazarus. People were everywhere, just waiting and watching, to see what would happen. When they heard what the young preacher said, they must have thought he was crazy. Maybe he was filled with the devil (as some had suggested.)

Then he called again, this time with even more authority than before, "Lazarus, come forth!"

The crowd began to mutter things like, "He's not hard of hearing; he's dead." The air became thick. Then, suddenly, there in the shadow of the doorway of the tomb, an image could be seen. It was someone bandaged from head to toe. But who was this shadowy figure? Was this some sort of hoax?

The young preacher spoke to some men standing nearby and told them to loose the person in the bandages. As the bandages were being removed from the body, everyone gasped. There before them was Lazarus, standing and crying with joy.

Martha ran to embrace her brother, and the Magdalen fell at the feet of the young preacher. "Praise be to God!" shouted many who were in the crowd. "Praise be to God!" Then Lazarus and Martha came and hugged and kissed the young preacher. For a moment, the Magdalene, Martha, Lazarus and he all stood there hugging each other, with tears flowing down their faces, and they, too, were saying, "Praise be to God! Praise be to God!" This was one of the most memorable and touching experiences of the young preacher's thirty-three-year life.

It's not over,

until it is all over.

But only God says

when it's all over!

—Anonymous

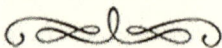

~11~

Ten Miles Away

A lot had taken place since the young preacher's cousin, a man known as John the Baptist, had baptized him in the Jordan River at Bethabara in Perea and a dove had descended upon him. That was where he first engaged John's disciples and then set out to assemble his own team. En route to Galilee, he was walking through the Judean desert when he was severely tempted by Satan.

The tempter knew that the young preacher was fasting in preparation to begin his ministry, so he offered him three different temptations. All three were declined. These were the same three temptations that are renounced during modern-day baptisms: the World, the Flesh and the Devil, otherwise known as the lust of the eyes, the lust of the flesh (body) and the pride of life. This refers to wanting something just because you have seen it, wanting something just because you think it would feel good, and, lastly, wanting something because you think others will think better of you for having it.

The young preacher trusted God to meet all his needs, just as he taught his disciples to do. After he had rebuffed the devil, God sent His angels to tend to his needs. He then continued on to Galilee and formed the core of the early Church. That's when the miracles began, and so, too, did the challenges.

The established order of the existing church was not thrilled about this new preacher and his message of faith and love. Not only had the raising of Lazarus been a profound moment in the young preacher's ministry; it also served as a tipping point for the religious order. Mary's brother being brought back to life in front of so many witnesses was more than they could bear.

~*~

As the fame of the young preacher grew, so did his detractors, who seemed to despise him. It was no secret that the Pharisees hated him, and he was not showing them a great deal of grace either. Their hatred for him was not merely sour grapes because of his notoriety. Nor was it for the simple reason that he was good and they were bad. They hated him because he threatened their security, their prestige and their way of life.

The Pharisees had brokered a business deal between the powers in Rome and their own people. This had made them the self-appointed voice of the people. No news was heard unless it came by and through them. But now everyone was talking about this young preacher who displayed such great power, power that previously only they had. This new preacher was jeopardizing their entire operation. His popularity, his talk of the kingdom having come, as well as the proclamation by many that he was the King of the Jews ... this was more than they could or would stomach.

The Pharisees hated the young preacher, not because he made them look bad in front of the people, but, rather, because he made them look bad in front of Rome. Word about him was bound to reach Rome soon, if it hadn't already. All this clamor about a messiah in their midst and a new king would certainly draw the ire of Roman authorities, which meant that they would come and deal with the situation personally, having lost all confidence in the incumbent religious rulers.

Sure enough, the news of what the young preacher had done for Lazarus spread quickly ... until everyone everywhere was buzzing that he was the messiah that had been prophesied for so long. Now the Pharisees and other religious leaders would have to act quickly. The yearly Passover feast, a time traditionally known for focusing on God's promise to deliver His people through a chosen messiah, was quickly approaching. It was evident that the people were ready to claim that this man was the chosen messiah and that prophecy was now being fulfilled through him. The decision was made to kill the young preacher before the people had a chance to present him to the world as the chosen one.

With the Passover now only a few days away, they frantically schemed to have him arrested and then killed—and Lazarus with him. This would remove any evidence that he was the chosen messiah. If they were able to kill him, it would prove that he was merely a man like any other.

~*~

Meanwhile, the young preacher was going about his ministry business as usual. He expressed a desire to meet with all of his disciples prior to the Passover, to give them insight as to what to expect in the coming days. It was determined that they would meet at Lazarus' and Martha's house in Bethany, as it was just a mile and a half outside of Jerusalem. The young preacher did not want to meet in the middle of Passover festivities.

As they all gathered in the house, before a word could be spoken, the Magdalene entered the crowded room and did something unusual.

CLOSE

The Magdalene made her way over to the young preacher with an alabaster jar cradled in her arms. Then she knelt down at his feet and gently began to wash them with the very expensive oil. Tears fell from her eyes as she thought of the goodness that God had shown her just days earlier by bringing her brother back from the dead. She was so grateful to Him for having healed her and her family.

The Magdalene used her long, lovely, dark hair to wipe the oil and tears from the preacher's feet. She kissed his feet and caressed them gently, as she said to him, "I love you, Lord. I love you. Thank you for all that you have done for me and my family."

This peaceful and tender worship of him was interrupted by one of her brother apostle's displeasure at her wasting such an expensive item just to wash someone's feet. "That was a waste of a very expensive item we could have sold for cash to help support the ministry," said Judas. Others chimed in, offering their suggestions for a better usage for the costly fragrance.

CLOSE

Someone suggested that the Magdalene might be reverting to her old ways of seduction, doing to him as she had done in the past with other men. Disgust and anger were rising in the room.

Sensing this, the young preacher asked, "Why are you bothering her? She has done a beautiful thing for me. You will always have others with needs, but you won't always have me.

"Have any among you ever washed my feet? Who greeted me with a kiss when they came in? Which of you has shown me your great love today?" The room fell silent.

The Magdalene then proceeded to pour the rest of the oil over his body as if to prepare him for burial. She had always listened so intently to his words, somehow believing that he would be leaving them soon. As others looked on with horror, the young preacher said, "This ... what she has done here today, will always be remembered. It will never ever be forgotten!" He had a great appreciation for the liberty with which the Magdalene pledged her allegiance and love for him. And his love for her, in return, was something very special.

In those moments, the Magdalene felt something very strong within telling her to cherish as never before these next few days before the Passover. Then the young preacher shared his preparation instructions, and they finished their dinner. The next few days would be challenging for all of them.

Turn your face
to the sun,
and the shadows
will fall behind you!

—Unknown

~12~

Two Miles Away

People from all over the country were coming to Jerusalem for the Passover Feast. It was one of the most popular events of the year, even more so now because of the extra excitement around hearing about the young preacher and the mighty works he was doing. The courtyard of the temple was sure to be packed every day of Passover week, with each person present hoping to get a glimpse of the chosen messiah. The atmosphere was electric.

The young preacher's resolve was greater than it had ever been. Ministry, ministry, ministry! This was the perfect time to showcase to all mankind the glory of God. He had prepared himself and his followers as best as he could for the days ahead. His plan was to spend each day ministering to the hundreds who would be present, teaching, sharing and loving them all.

The next morning, after everyone had risen, he gave special instructions to two of his followers. He told them that a man had offered his mule and colt to them to aid their travel back and forth to the Passover. They should go bring them. The two went and did as the young preacher had requested.

When they returned with the animals, they proceeded to cover their backs with cloaks and tunics (neither animal had come with a saddle). Now, everything was in place for the whole group to enter the city for Passover week.

~*~

Word had quickly gotten out that the young preacher was staying at Bethany in the home of Lazarus. Upon hearing this news, crowds began strategically positioning themselves on the road from Bethany to the temple in hopes of getting a glimpse of him.

When the young preacher and his disciples got near the city, they saw hundreds of people on both sides of the road, all the way to the Outer Court of the temple. Just as the palm trees were lining the road, so, too, were the people. Many had pulled branches from the trees and now began waving them as he came near, and their were cries of "Hosanna, Hosanna, blessed is he that cometh in the name of the Lord, even the King of Israel."

As these praises filled the air, the Magdalene and the other disciples were astonished at what was happening and began looking around in awe. So many people, filled with so much hope! Many in the multitude had witnessed what the young preacher did for Lazarus at the tomb. Others had either seen or heard of some of the other miracles that had taken place. For the disciples, it was a lot to take in. But the preacher knew that prophecy was being fulfilled right in front of their eyes.

More palm branches were raised and more cries now emanated from the throng as the procession got closer to the temple. Some began spreading fine garments on the ground where the party traveled, a sign of respect for royalty.

By now the crowd had grown to hundreds. Interspersed among those who cheered were also some haters, among them some Pharisees who had taken notice of the spectacle that was before them. They now urged the young preacher to stop the people from praising and worshiping him as though he were God.

In reply, the young preacher gave a quick retort: "If they don't cry out, then the rocks most definitely will!"

The Pharisees must have thought to themselves, "Both he and the world seem to have gone mad. What shall we do?"

With so many people present, I imagine it did feel like the whole world was there watching.

Another group also opposed this apparent coronation. They were the Sadducees. They were not quite as concerned because they had a plan of their own, a reception of a different sort for the would-be king!

The young preacher, feeling the rejection of those around him, began to weep for the city. He was heard saying that because the city had not accepted him fully as the Savior, it would soon be utterly destroyed. Soon enough, the procession would arrive at the temple.

~*~

Meanwhile a group of believers who were not common to that area were inquiring about the young preacher. This group had traveled all the way from Egypt just to see the supposed

Messiah. They were unusual in that they were Hellenistic Jews, those who were living the Greek culture while practicing Jewish traditions. Often misunderstood, they felt that if they could just get to the Messiah, then revelation would be imminent. They came across Phillip and Andrew in the crowd and made their request known, to see the young preacher. When they told the young preacher, he was moved by their perseverance and sat down with them in the temple to teach them the principles of the Kingdom of God.

He also began to share with this group his purpose for coming to the Passover festivities. While he was yet speaking with them, a loud sound, almost like thunder, was heard. Then suddenly the heavens opened up, and the people around the preacher heard him say, "Now my soul is troubled, but what shall I say? Father, save me from this hour? But for this very purpose I have come to this hour. Father, glorify Your name!"

Then they heard another sound. A strong voice answered, "I have already glorified it, and I will glorify it again."

Those who were gathered around tried to figure out what they had just heard. Some said it was only thunder. Others said it was an angel speaking to the preacher. He said, "The voice did not come on my behalf but, rather, for your sake."

After that, he left the temple and headed for a place of retreat, to seclude himself. The disciples stood there bewildered at what had just happened. The Magdalene said that what they had just witnessed was God the Father letting them know the time had come for the young preacher to be offered up as The Passover Lamb. The others found this saying to be even more puzzling than what they had already seen and heard. Some of them felt that the Magdalene was out of place in saying what she did, and resentment of her lingered.

"She is a woman entirely out of her place," some thought to themselves. "She is trying to upstage us." But, in

CLOSE

her heart, the motives of the Magdalene were pure. She just wanted to share the insight she had been given with the rest of the team. She just wanted to help.

Passover is a time of reflection and joy,
when we emerge from our cocoon of doubt
to fly freely on the wings of faith.

—Unknown

One Hundred Feet Away

Later that evening the Magdalene went for a walk like she had done so many other nights before, but this night was different. She felt different. Things were different. She felt the displeasure of her fellow ministers, as well as the heartache of possibly losing the Messiah, her Rabboni.

She always referred to him as "Rabboni" as a sign of honor and reverence, Rabboni meaning "Master and Teacher." That was who he was to her. For his part, he was always very appreciative of her care for him.

She thought that perhaps the sweet soothing smell of the Mountain Lavender Lily would help to put her soul at ease. As she strolled down a pathway, she picked a few lilies and found a place to rest. While seated, she began to reflect on the events of the past few days. The more she thought, the fuller her heart became, and the more she wept. She began praying in earnest for the young preacher because she sensed what was about to come to him.

Some time passed, and she was joined by Thomas and Matthew, who had come to check on her. As the three of them began reflecting on the events of the day, the young preacher came to where they were. He shared with them that the time had come for him to rest.

They said to him, "Please, Lord, have a seat." They thought perhaps he was fatigued from the hustle and bustle of the day. But he went on to tell them exactly what he meant by "rest." He explained to them that he had come to open the path and teach them how to travel through it. That path was to know the Father in Heaven. "When you pray to Him," he explained, "say, 'Hear us, just as You heard Your only begotten Son.' "

The young preacher gave them deeper insights and revelations regarding the days to come. Once he finished, he asked if they had understood what he was telling them. Thomas and Matthew expressed their confusion at the things he had said, but the Magdalene spoke up and said, "Rabboni, I believe I understand."

He said to her, "Please speak, dear daughter."

The Magdalene began to share the fact that many thought the Rabboni had come to be an earthly king who would overthrow the Roman Empire. "I believe that you have come," she said, "to shift the focus from earth to Heaven, to teach us that we should put more focus on Heaven and heavenly things than we do on the earthly.

CLOSE

Far too much of our time is focused on things that aren't eternal. Your Kingdom is eternal.

"This is the day when we select the lamb to be presented at Passover, and this day, Heaven has selected You, my Rabboni, as the Lamb of God. Behold, the Lamb of God!"

The young preacher smiled and said to the other two disciples, "The Magdalene is absolutely correct. Her revelation is from Heaven." And in that moment, she became an apostle to the apostles.

The Magdalene truly had a gift to understand the young preacher more than any of the other disciples, and her gift made their bond that much stronger and brought them that much close.

The hour had drawn late, and they all needed to get some rest for the days to come. So they went back to Lazarus' house to spend the night.

~*~

The young preacher knew his days were now few, so he purposed that every day he would teach in the synagogues. The Magdalene purposed that everywhere he went, she would be his faithful companion. And so it was that everywhere he went the Magdalene was right there by his side.

When morning light came, the

CLOSE

young preacher began to wake the disciples so they could begin their day. The Magdalene was right by his side helping him to awaken the others. There was a certain expectancy in the air, given the fact that there were only a few hours left before Passover. They all sensed that this Passover would be unlike any they had ever experienced before.

Life is change.
Growth is optional.
Choose wisely!
— Unknown

When they reached the temple, merchants had set up their wares to sell to all those coming for Passover. The young preacher was furious and drove them out. He called them "a den of thieves." He recited the scripture passage, " 'My house will be a house of prayer,' says the Lord God." He ministered tirelessly to those who came to the temple that day.

On their evening walk back to Bethany, someone asked a question about the treatment of those who were trying to make an honest living by working at the temple. The young preacher responded by asking the group if anyone could explain what had happened that day. Peter, James and John had nothing to say and nor did most of the others.

The Magdalene offered her insights. "Rabboni, were they driven out because God's house is a place for worship and not a place for personal gain or advancement? Our sole purpose for coming to the temple is to give God His due glory for the things He has done in our lives."

The young preacher confirmed her by adding, "The apostle has correctly understood what happened." Some didn't like the fact that she had spoken and was received and confirmed by him.

That night the young preacher and the Magdalene walked together.

The Magdalene knew that the time was close for the Lamb of God to be sacrificed. Although it was difficult for her emotionally, and many times she felt like crying, she knew she had to be strong and supportive for him. It was imperative to her that he not feel alone during this time.

Some of the other disciples did not appreciate the closeness the two shared. Peter and Judas in particular were quite outspoken about their feelings against this relationship. They later used it as a provocation for their own misdeeds of betrayal and denial. But their actions only strengthened the bond between the young preacher and the Magdalene.

CLOSE

With each passing day, they drew ever closer to their intertwined eternal destiny.

~14~

Fifty Feet Away

The Passover was swiftly approaching, and so, too, were the plans to make it one of the most memorable in history. One group of planners consisted of seventy-one rabbis, known as the Great Sanhedrin. These men were working on their own special surprise.

As a group of religious judges, they had been around for a long time, dating back to the days of Moses, when the Israelites were commanded by God to establish order among the people. Their group had overseen the temple in Jerusalem and legislated all aspects of Jewish religious and political matters for the past several decades. Their plan to establish order this time included killing the young preacher. They didn't know just how or when they would do it, but they knew he must go.

At the same time, there was some dissention among the followers of the young preacher. Not everyone agreed with his coronation program. Judas wanted him to rule all of Judea and overthrow Rome with the use of generals and armies. "Certainly I and the other disciples would make great generals," Judas must have thought to himself. The young preacher's plan for kingship was far less assertive than the one Judas envisioned. "Maybe he just needed a little prodding," Judas thought. "Then, he will see things my way."

The Sanhedrin confided in Judas their plan to arrest the young preacher and put him on trial. Judas thought this was the perfect incentive to cause the preacher to invoke his authority and take over as king. So Judas and the members of the Sanhedrin entered into a contract, with the "where" and "when" to be decided.

While all of this was taking place, the young preacher and the Magdalene were off to themselves again on a quiet walk.

The Magdalene asked her Rabboni if they could stop and talk for a while because she had something on her heart she wanted to share with him. He agreed.

The Magdalene began to share with him a vision that she had. She really didn't know whether she was awake or in a pre-sleep state when she had the vision, she said, but she saw him.

The preacher lightheartedly commented that it was good she hadn't fainted or wavered when she saw him. "Where the mind is," he said, "that's where one's treasure is."

"Rabboni," she said, leaving the details of the vision for a moment, "does a vision come through a person's soul or their spirit?"

CLOSE

He answered, "I don't see it as being through the soul or the spirit. When two people have the same mindset, that is where a vision comes from. Our like-mindedness is what brings us together."

Let this mind be in you,
which was also in Christ.

— Philippians 2:5[7]

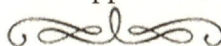

While pondering these things in her heart, the Magdalene continued sharing her vision.

"Rabboni, it was as if I saw you returning from a journey you had been on. I'm not certain where you had

7. The Holy Bible, King James Version, public domain

gone, but it appeared to be somewhere 'down.' I know that sounds a bit odd, but that's what I saw."

He urged her to continue, and she did. "I didn't see you going down, but I did see you coming up. It seem as if you had just traveled through what I believe were seven stages or seven worlds. Each one of them was more wicked and wearying than the last, yet you remained strong in faith. I'm not certain what it all means.

"I don't know whether this was in my thoughts or in my spirit," continued the Magdalene. "Will you help me discern it, Rabboni?"

The young preacher paused and told her that what she had experienced was given to her in her spirit from the Chief Spirit, Father God. "Daughter," he said, "truly you have been favored with insight from above. No one knows the day or hour, not the angels in Heaven or even the Son, but only the Father. The Father has shown you what no other eyes have seen. In His time, more will be revealed to you."

After the young preacher spoke these words, there was only silence. No animals, no birds, no insects, no wind, nothing spoke.

~*~

On the morrow was the day before Passover, and the young preacher had planned to get together with all of his disciples for a pre-Passover meal, so he directed some of his followers to go and secure an upper room that had been prepared for them in the home of Mary the mother of the disciple named John Mark. This was a customary meeting place for the followers located inside the walls of Jerusalem, in an area which had palatial homes and some very affluent residents. He wanted them to make sure that everything was set for all who would be in attendance—his mother, the women who had come with him from Galilee, some close supporters in Jerusalem and the rest of the disciples.

CLOSE

While all the preparations were being settled, the young preacher and the Magdalene went off quietly to themselves again. "Rabboni," she said, "I've received more on the vision just as you said I would. May I share it with you?"

He smiled and nodded yes.

"Here is what I saw regarding the seven worlds. The first world was obsessed with darkness. There was no light at all in that realm, nor did many of its residents want any.

"The second world was constructed of desire, where every evil of the hearts of men was manifested to the highest form.

"The third world was one of sheer ignorance. People everywhere were perishing because of their lack of knowledge.

"The fourth world was constructed by a zeal for death. Everyone was moving so quickly and not paying attention to the signs to slow down and observe.

"The fifth world was a realm where the flesh ruled. Everything was about self-consumption, and no regard was given for anything other than one's self.

"Through each realm I saw you fighting to free the souls of those who received you and your message of the Kingdom of Heaven, and in each realm, your following increased more and more.

CLOSE

"Next came the sixth world, the world of foolish wisdom. In this world, people were leaning toward their own personal experiences or understandings about life, where no truth was higher than their own.

"The last and final world that I saw you come up through was the world of the wisdom of the wrathful or hurt ones. No one was willing to forgive anyone for anything. As with each of the other realms, you were able to set those captives free that received you and your word.

"All this I saw in a vision, Rabboni. While all these things were quite fantastic, the one thing that puzzled me the most was that all this was done after you were dead. Please tell me what it means."

"Daughter," he responded, "what you have seen is the future. I will die, and I will go to the depths of Hades and free the lost souls. Each world represents the nature of man. This is a great thing that you have been shown.

"And we truly are close! What has bound me has now been slain, what surrounds me has been overcome, my desire has been ended, and all ignorance has died. I have been released from this world, and it is time for a new season.

"From this hour on, my due season is upon me because my Father has shown you the things to come. Soon it will be your turn, and the others, your time to go forth and proclaim the Good News of the Kingdom of Heaven."

The Magdalene took these words into her heart and prayed about them in the days that followed.

Prayer is the most important conversation of the day

—Unknown

Ten Feet Away

The evening had come, and the young preacher and his invited guests were all gathering in the upper room in the house of John Mark's mother Mary, for their Seder meal. After everyone had arrived, he thanked them for coming and for the support they had always given him. He prayed and asked God to bless them for their efforts.

As the preacher broke a loaf of bread to share with the rest of them, he began speaking about what the next few days would hold for him. He had their undivided attention. He shared that he had been eagerly awaiting this moment to eat the Passover meal with them before he suffered.

In defense of him, Peter said, "We will not let anyone harm you, Lord."

The young preacher continued, "Yes, one of you who sits here tonight with us will betray me, and I shall be killed. The burden of this is quite heavy. I will go to the garden and pray to my Father for the strength to endure this moment."

Upon hearing this, each disciple began defending their own honor by claiming their personal greatness and importance to the ministry. He urged them all not to enter into temptation through being distracted, but the clamor continued.

In the middle of all the confusion of this conversation, Judas slipped out of the room. "If the young preacher is ever to be convinced to take the throne of Rome, the time is now," he must have been thinking to himself. So he went to speak with the members of the Sanhedrin and tell them where they could find the messiah whom they sought. He went to tell them where the young preacher would be next and that he would personally point him out to them.

Meanwhile, as the others finished their Seder meal, they began singing hymns and praising the Lord on their way out to the Mount of Olives to pray. The young preacher now offered some parting words. "I already know that each of you will be ashamed of me this night. You will draw back from me, for it has been written in the Scriptures: 'The Shepherd will be struck, and the flock shall be scattered.' I understand that it will happen. But after I am raised up, I will see you again in Galilee."

Peter assured the Lord that he could never be ashamed of him. The young preacher insisted that not only would he, in a short time, be ashamed of him, but he would also deny that he had ever known him.

CLOSE

The young preacher proceeded from there to a place where olives were pressed and mashed into olive oil, a place called Gethsemane. He was now full of sorrow about what was about to happen and even seemed to be very weak in his body.

Just as he had predicted, Judas betrayed him to the Sanhedrin council members, and they came to arrest the young preacher, carrying with them clubs and swords. As foretold, he would be brutally beaten and tortured again and again, all through the night, and then, early in the morning, he was taunted further still with a mock trial.

When all of this transpired, the disciples were in shock and went into hiding. No one spoke on his behalf and just fifteen hours after their last Seder with him, he was to be executed for treason. These men were fearful that they might be next, and the women were utterly heartbroken because of the cruelty being shown to their Savior.

Anger ends in cruelty!

— Unknown

The crucifixion was set to begin at nine o' clock in the morning on the Hill of Golgotha, which means "the place of the skull," just outside of Jerusalem. It was also called

Calavera, or "the bald skull." This little hill stood in stark contrast to the mighty Mount Hermon.

~*~

One of the many miraculously historical moments the Messiah and the great Mount Hermon had shared was that of his transfiguration. In that moment, the young preacher's earthly body had been transformed into a glorious heavenly body. The glory of the Lord had been upon him, and he had not been alone. Others witnessed the event.

In his efforts to draw others close, he had called Peter, James and

John to join him on one of his many times of worship and prayer on the mountain. He began his worship that day thanking God as he had always done for the many blessings and favors that had been bestowed upon his life.

Then, as his praise and adoration had increased, the glow of the joy of the Lord appeared on his face, and God's glory began to compass him about. His face was illuminated, and his clothes were glowing with God's glory and approval of him.

Then the heavens began to open, and bright beams of light began to shine down on him. This light was so bright that the disciples had to cover their eyes and shield their faces.

CLOSE

When the light eventually toned down and the men were able to reopen their eyes, they saw three figures standing where there had previously only been one. The young preacher had been joined in this time of worship by Moses and Elijah.

Moses represented God's Law being given to His people, Elijah represented God's Prophecy being given to His people, and the young preacher represented the fulfillment of all of God's Promises given both in word and prophecy. All three were there praising God together for the fulfillment of His Word.

Hermon's peak was so close to Heaven that day that two of Heaven's most prominent citizens had decided to join the young preacher's worship celebration of the Almighty. Truly Mount Hermon was a very special place.

* * *

In a world

where everyone wears a mask,

it's nice to see a soul!

—Unknown

* * *

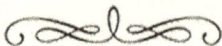

Peter, James and John hadn't fully grasped that day the depth of significance of what they had witnessed. Peter, his senses overwhelmed, had suggested that they should build three temples, one for each of them right there on the spot where they had stood, to commemorate this special occasion.

Then, suddenly, out of a bright cloud had come these words: "This is My Son; listen to Him!"

Upon hearing this, the disciples had fallen to the ground on their faces. The young preacher had touched them and said, "It's okay; let's be going."

When they had looked up, they only saw the preacher. Moses and Elijah were gone. The disciples were so astonished and amazed by what they had just experienced that they would never forget it.

On Hermon, where the transfiguration occurred, his clothes had become white as light, while on Golgotha's hill, the soldiers desecrated his garments, ripping them off of him. Moses and Elijah had accompanied him on Hermon, but now two thieves were crucified on either side of him at the hill of Golgotha. Hermon heard declarations from Heaven and Father God about who the young preacher was, while, at Golgotha, the crowd screamed out, "Crucify him!"

As he hung on the cross for hours, at his feet were the faithful: the Magdalene, his mother and her step-sister Mary Salome, along with many other women believers. They were still pleading and begging for God to intervene, but that was not His plan.

CLOSE

Even the young preacher himself, in a moment of weakness, asked if God had forsaken him. Then, finally, he prayed and said, "It is finished!" And, with that, he bowed his head in solemn surrender and released his spirit from his body. The Father's plan had been fulfilled.

At that very instant, Hermon marked this momentous occasion as only he could. In unison, all the volcanoes that rested on his age-old back erupted, spewing upward thick black ash that completely covered the sky, completely blocking out the sun, while downward he caused earthquakes that shook the world to its core—both actually and figuratively.

As the earth rumbled, many of the nearby sepulchres were destroyed, and buildings shifted and tumbled to the ground. In that moment, someone uttered, "Surely this must have been the Son of God." Everything and everyone was shaken and would never be the same again.

~*~

A secret but devout believer named Joseph, accompanied by a man named Nicodemus, received special permission to remove the young preacher's body from the cross. In this, they were aided by John, his mother Mary, Mary Salome, the Magdalene and several other women who were present. All of them were heartbroken to see and hold the beaten, bloody and emaciated body of their Savior.

As they carried his body to the tomb that had been secured for his burial, the Magdalene began rubbing oil on his body. She and the other women were praying over him continually. This was a very sad moment for all.

They laid him in the stone tomb and covered his body with an expensive linen burial cloth. The suggestion was made that they place a heavy stone in front of the entrance so as not to allow curious onlookers to disrupt the burial site. Also, as a precautionary measure, to prevent any further rebellion, the governor ordered the tomb to be guarded by a battalion of Roman soldiers.

The young preacher's mother, Mary, had to be helped to her feet by John and the Magdalene while she was departing from the tomb.

That evening John went out searching for the rest of the apostles to gather them all in one place. He was eventually able to locate them all. He told them to meet him in two days' time at the same upper room where they had held their last Seder with the young preacher. This would allow for some of the emotions to cool down and things to perhaps settle a bit.

CLOSE

People were everywhere in the streets looting and looking for mischief. There were also those who were looking for the followers of the young preacher for guidance and direction after the day's events. Others were looking for the disciples to do them harm because of their involvement with the rebel rouser they called the Messiah. Emotions were heightened all around.

Meanwhile, back in her home, the Magdalene and others continued consoling Mary over the loss of her son. Everyone was very bewildered and full of disbelief. No one knew what to do or what would happen next. Would there be an effort to gather all those involved in the young preacher's ministry and also cause them harm? Would they also be killed? Would they be exiled? No one knew what would happen. Many felt that the outlook for the future was quite bleak. The brightest hope they had ever seen was now gone, taken from their midst. Their leader was dead. It truly seemed as though all hope was gone.

Eventually Mary was able to gain some level of peace and attempt to rest. Others continued to remain by her side to comfort her.

Some walks

You have to take alone!

—Unknown

~16~

Five Feet Away

As she had done customarily before, the Magdalene went for a walk. Her heart was very heavy, for she no longer had the accompaniment of her Rabboni. The days were long and empty for her. The ache of a lost loved one was quite extreme, like a huge stone that sat on her chest and heart. The hours seemed to crawl by, hours that felt like a week had passed.

As she walked through the black soot ash from the eruptions, she kept thinking about her last days with the Rabboni. Somehow battling through her feelings of great loss, she began to pray. She resorted back to the things that her Rabboni had shown and taught them.

She prayed for his mother and siblings, prayed for his followers and prayed for all the people he had served and died for. She prayed for the Kingdom and the work of the Lord to continue. She prayed and prayed. Like her Rabboni, she resolved to pray all night and all day. Each morning she would begin her day and each evening end her day at his gravesite.

CLOSE

The grieving process would be long and hard. There were times when she and Mary would go together as therapy for the both of them. It was unfathomable that he was gone. It felt like a dream or a bad nightmare that they couldn't wake up from.

The Magdalene often reflected on some of her last conversations alone with the Rabboni. She remembered one of the last things he had said to her when she told him about her vision. She recalled how she had seen him traveling for days through various regions and places to free others who were held captive. Deep within her soul, she believed that her Rabboni was doing this work now. Somehow, somewhere he was helping those who were lost. He was still doing Kingdom work.

~*~

Two days had now passed, and the time had come for the disciples to meet again since the capture and crucifixion. No one knew what to expect. Gradually, one by one, the apostles began entering the upper room. Their anxiety level was still quite high. Had they been followed there? Did anyone see them entering? Everyone was still so afraid and confused at the events of Passover. What exactly had happened? And how and wy had it happened?

CLOSE

Noticeably absent from the group was the Magdalene, Thomas and Judas. The Magdalene, they knew, was with his mother Mary, offering her comfort during this horrible time. But what of Thomas and Judas? Where were they? Were they together? Had they been taken as well? Did they know something that no one else did?

Speculations quickly turned toward those unaccounted for as possible partakers in the young preacher's demise. Were they responsible? Someone mentioned the fact that they overheard someone say that Judas had met with the Sanhedrin in a secret closed-door meeting. What was that about? This news only fueled and heightened their suspicions about him. He had always been so jealous and greedy! "We all know how he loved money," someone said. "Maybe they offered him something!"

The panic was thick in the room. Who would be next? Would they each be taken, one by one, or would they come for all of them at once? Surely whoever betrayed him would no doubt betray them also. Some of them wanted to leave that place and go into hiding in another country or far-away land. They all decided it was best to stay together, at least until the next morning. Maybe tomorrow, the third day, which fell on the Holy Sabbath, some new light would be shed on everything.

CLOSE

There is nothing uncertain
but the uncertain!
—Unknown

The Magdalene got up that next morning and headed to the tomb, just as she had been doing every day. Can you understand what a person feels when a good friend is suddenly gone, the loneliness, the heartache, the sense of loss? Those feelings were multiplied a hundred times for the Magdalene, given that the young preacher was not only her friend, but also her Rabboni and Savior as well. He was, she was convinced, the Son of God!

It was this thought that gave her the most optimism. It wasn't over yet. It couldn't be over yet! He was not dead. Maybe he was simply asleep like her brother Lazarus had been.

It was the Holy Sabbath, the dawn of the first day of a new week, so the Magdalene, her friend and fellow disciple, Joanna, the young preacher's mother and her sister, Mary Salome, were all going to the tomb. They had work to do. They had gathered spices to anoint his body, and now they set off on the more than two-mile walk to the tomb. On their way they discussed how the stone would get rolled away. They were resolved to the fact that God would make a way for them.

CLOSE

As they approached the tomb, they noticed that there were no Roman soldiers standing guard, and the stone had already been rolled away from the entrance of the tomb. "What could have happened?" they wondered to themselves. "Where were the soldiers? Who moved the stone?"

The Magdalene stepped inside the tomb to look for her Rabboni's body, but it was not there. What had they done with him? Where had they moved his body? She began weeping for fear that someone had taken him away.

Then she noticed two men dressed in white who were just standing there. They asked her why she was weeping.

She said, "Because they have taken My Lord somewhere."

Thinking that one of them was a gardener, she asked, "Do you know where they took him?"

He then said, "Mary, the Magdalene," and she knew that voice. She immediately fell at his feet and cried, "My Rabboni, it is you!"

Everything within her wanted to embrace him and never let him go. He knew this, but he told her she could not touch him yet. He said he needed to go to his Father first.

She expressed how glad she was to see him. He showed the same joy at seeing her. He told her to go and tell the rest of the disciples what she had seen. He said he would meet them on a nearby mountain shortly. The Magdalene and the other women ran quickly to tell the others what they had seen and heard.

When they reached the upper room, they ran inside to share the good news. To their amazement, no one believed what they were saying. Some thought the women had been tricked. Or perhaps they were delusional, given all that had happened. Peter spoke up and said, "Let's go see for ourselves." So off they went.

When Peter and the others arrived at the tomb, he, too, saw that the stone had been rolled away, the soldiers were gone, and the body of the young preacher was missing. Nothing remained but the burial linen cloth that he had been wrapped in. With everyone looking perplexed, the Magdalene reminded them that the Rabboni had said he would meet them on the mountain. The word was quickly spreading that the young preacher had risen.

As the disciples reached the mountain, so, too, did hundreds of other believers. According to the accounts, more than five hundred others were there to witness the resurrected Lord. When the disciples saw him, they began to worship him, singing praises to God for this miracle. However, there were still some doubters among them.

CLOSE

The risen Lord spoke and said to them, "All authority in Heaven and earth has been given to me. Go therefore and make disciples in all nations. Baptize them in the name of the Father, the Son and the Holy Spirit, teaching them to practice all that I have shown you. I will be with you always even unto the end of time." Then he departed from that place.

Through the doors of perception,
down the corridors of uncertainty,
into the room of self doubt,
opens the window of opportunity!

—Unknown

~17~

One Foot Away

The disciples were afraid to go out and preach because they saw how their master had been killed because of it. "If they killed him, then they will certainly kill us too!" they lamented. The Magdalene stepped forward and said, "Don't be worried. He promised he would be with us to protect us."

As their hearts turned, they began to remember and discuss his teachings. Peter asked the Magdalene to tell them some of the things she had heard or knew that the rest of them did not. "Sister," he said, "we know that the Savior loved you more than he did the rest of the women. Tell us more of the things you remember." He did this out of envy and jealousy, but the Magdalene agreed.

"I will tell you some things that have been hidden from you," she began, and started telling them about her vision of the Rabboni traveling through other kingdoms or worlds and setting the captives free in them. She explained how he had gone into Sheol and then gone up to Heaven. Finally, she spoke of her private conversations with the Rabboni regarding the vision.

CLOSE

Sharing the fact that she had asked the Rabboni whether one saw a vision through their soul or through their spirit and that he had answered her that she saw him through her mind, she suggested that they were close in their thoughts. That statement aroused some controversy in the room. Was she closer to the Messiah than the rest of them? She was sharing teachings that they had never heard from him!

Now Peter chimed in. "Are we all supposed to listen to her now? Did he speak secretly with a woman and not openly to us? Are we to believe that he preferred her over us? Is she suggesting that we forget all that he told us and listen to her?"

The Magdalene began to cry and said to Peter, "Brother, do you think I am just making this up? Why would I lie about the Rabboni?"

Matthew stepped up to defend the Magdalene's honor and stop the attack. "Say what you will," he said, "I believe the Savior said these things to her." He reiterated how she alone among all of the disciples had remained faithfully by his side during the trial and the crucifixion. He went on to tell how she was also the first one he showed himself to once he had risen from the tomb. "The Lord told her to tell us to come here. She is special! They are close!"

Over the next forty days or so, the preacher appeared to numerous people in that area and continued to share the message of the Kingdom of Heaven, often with the Magdalene right by his side. A legend states that the Magdalene remained among the early believers for more than a decade, sharing the Gospel of the Kingdom.

When James was executed in Jerusalem, the Magdalene, her sister Martha, her brother Lazarus and other believers were persecuted and imprisoned because of preaching the Gospel. The Jewish leaders were afraid that if they executed this group the crowd would be uncontrollable. So they placed them on a boat without sails, oars or supplies and set them adrift on the ocean to die. Hermon watched over them as the ship floated out of sight into the open sea. They had an intertwined eternal destiny—the Messiah, the Mountain and the Magdalene.

Narrowly escaping death many times on their voyage, the group landed in the south of France, over two thousand miles from Jerusalem. The Magdalene, along with the other believers, brought many souls into the knowledge of the Kingdom of Heaven. The Rabboni never left her side. She remained Close!